There are flies in the house.

Pesky, buzzing, annoying flies, in the house.

Are they in the living room?

Yes, one fly in the Livingroom.

Are they in the kitchen?

Yes, one, two, 2 flies in the kitchen.

That's two, three flies in the house.

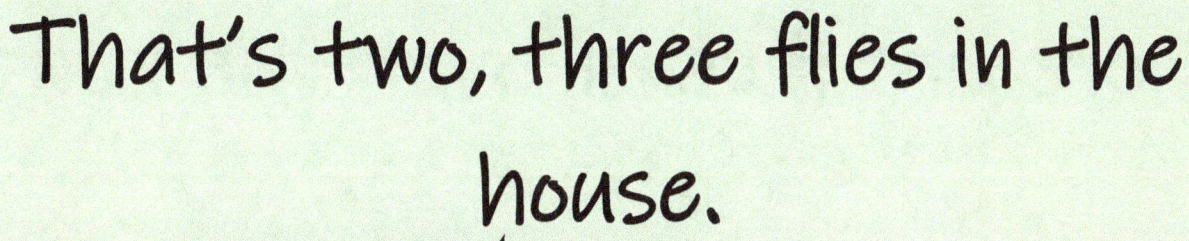

There are flies all over the house.

Are there flies in the bedroom?

Oh, gosh! One fly in the bedroom.

Four flies in the house.

Is the bathroom safe from flies?

Oh no, there is one fly there, too.

Five flies in the house.

what to do, what to do, with the 5 flies, all over the house.

Smack, one fly in the bathroom,

4 flies to go.

Swat, the fly in the bedroom,
3 flies to go.

Squish and squash, no more flies in the kitchen,

only 1 more fly in the house.

Where could that fly be?

Ssswwaaatt

1

No more pesky, buzzing, annoying flies.

www.ingramcontent.com/pod-product-compliance
Lightning Source LLC
Chambersburg PA
CBHW082249300426
44110CB00039B/2487